LADY GAGA

by E. Merwin

Consultant: Starshine Roshell
Music and Entertainment Journalist
Santa Barbara, California

BEARPORT PUBLISHING

New York, New York

Credits

Cover, © Everett Collection Inc./Alamy; 4, © Hahn Lionel/ABAC USA/Newscom; 5, © PG Splash News/ Newscom; 6, © Seth Poppel Yearbook Library; 7, Courtesy Beyond My Ken/Wikimedia Commons; 8, © Seth Poppel Yearbook Library; 9, © Rodrigo Reyes Marin/AFLO/Newscom; 10, Courtesy SPG; 11, © Philip Scalia/ Alamy Stock Photo; 12, © Sbukley/Dreamstime; 13, © Roger Wiliams/ZUMA Press/Newscom; 14, © Rich Graessle/Icon Sportswire/Newscom; 15, © Nicky Loh/Reuters/Newscom; 17, © Anwar Hussein Collection/ Newscom; 19, © David Sims/WENN.com/Newscom; 20, © AP Photo/Charles Krupa; 21, © Evan Agostini/ Invision/AP; 22T, © PG Splash News/Newscom; 22B, © Artur Yossundara/Dreamstime; 23, © Splash News/ Alamy Stock Photo.

Publisher: Kenn Goin
Creative Director: Spencer Brinker
Production and Photo Research: Shoreline Publishing Group LLC

Library of Congress Cataloging-in-Publication Data

Names: Merwin, E. author. | Roshell, Starshine.
Title: Lady Gaga / by E. Merwin ; consultant: Starshine Roshell.
Description: New York, New York : Bearport Publishing, 2019. | Series:
  Amazing Americans: Pop music stars | Includes bibliographical references
  and index.
Identifiers: LCCN 2018011086 (print) | LCCN 2018012369 (ebook) |
  ISBN 9781684027231 (Ebook) | ISBN 9781684026777 (library)
Subjects: LCSH: Lady Gaga—Juvenile literature. | Singers—United
  States—Biography—Juvenile literature.
Classification: LCC ML3930.L13 (ebook) | LCC ML3930.L13 M47 2019 (print) |
  DDC 782.42164092 [B] —dc23
LC record available at https://lccn.loc.gov/2018011086

For more information, write to Bearport Publishing Company, Inc., 45 West 21st Street, Suite 3B, New York, New York 10010. Printed in the United States of America.

10 9 8 7 6 5 4 3 2 1

CONTENTS

All Eyes on Gaga

Around the world, 150 million fans were watching. All eyes were on Lady Gaga! Shimmering in her costume, she flew on cables down to the stage. Then, Lady Gaga began to sing. It was the 2017 Super Bowl, and she was the shining star!

Lady Gaga was lowered from the top of the stadium.

Lady Gaga began the show by singing "God Bless America."

New Yorker

Lady Gaga was born in New York City on March 28, 1986. Her real name is Stefani Joanne Angelina Germanotta. At four years old, she began playing the piano. Every week, she practiced the piano and singing. When Stefani was 13, she wrote her first song. Two years later, she was on television for the first time!

Stefani as a child

New York City's Lee Strasberg Theatre where Stefani took acting classes

As a kid, Stefani studied acting every Saturday.

"Bullying Is for Losers"

In high school, Stefani loved to study. She also enjoyed singing and dancing in **musicals**. Some kids were jealous. They made fun of her for being different. Today, Lady Gaga tells her fans, "Bullying is for losers." She says, "Be true to who you are!"

Stefani as a high schooler

Lady Gaga has a nickname for her fans. She calls them her "little monsters."

Homework

After high school, Stefani studied acting at New York University (NYU). One evening at the school's library, she felt **inspired** to write a song. She worked for hours. By the time the library closed, Stefani had written "LoveGame." It became a song on her first album, *The Fame*, in 2008.

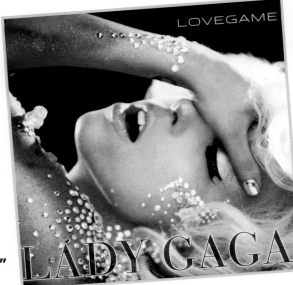

The song "LoveGame" came out in 2008.

This library at NYU is just one of the places where Lady Gaga wrote songs.

Sometimes, while washing dishes at home, Lady Gaga comes up with a new song idea!

The Fame

In 2010, *The Fame* won a **Grammy**! Around the world, fans loved dancing to the album's catchy beats and lyrics. Songs on the album, such as "Just Dance," were one of a kind— just like Lady Gaga!

"Just Dance" was made into a video game. It has sold over 25 million copies worldwide!

Here, Lady Gaga shows off one of her cool costumes during a show in San Diego.

13

Topping the Charts

Lady Gaga's "little monsters" were
eagerly waiting for her second album.
In 2011, *Born This Way* went on sale. In
one week, it sold over one million copies!
Topping the **charts**, the album was
a number one hit in 25 countries!

Lady Gaga wears
fun outfits whenever
she performs.

Wearing still another outrageous outfit, Lady Gaga speaks to reporters before a 2011 concert.

Lady Gaga has gone on five world tours. She has sold over 27 million albums.

Meeting the Queen

In 2009, Gaga performed for Queen Elizabeth II. Playing a piano raised 10 feet (3 m) above the stage, Lady Gaga sang "Speechless." Everyone talked about the strange red dress she wore. Like a balloon, it was made of rubbery latex!

"Speechless" is a song Lady Gaga had written for her dad.

The queen and
Lady Gaga

17

At the White House

Lady Gaga's stardom was growing each year. In 2013, President Barack Obama invited Gaga to the White House! She wore a huge white gown. First, she sang "You and I" from the album *Born This Way*. Then, Gaga was joined by the singer Tony Bennett for a **duet**. The pair later made an album together.

Lady Gaga first visited the White House in 2011. She talked about ways to stop bullying.

In London in 2014, Tony Bennett and Lady Gaga perform songs from their album, *Cheek to Cheek.*

A Kinder World

Gaga cares about more than just music. She and her mother, Cynthia, started a **foundation** called Born This Way. The group helps young people to feel special and strong. Lady Gaga says it best: "We can make the world a kinder and braver place."

Lady Gaga began her foundation with an event in 2012. Oprah Winfrey and other famous people came to the event to support her.

Lady Gaga and her mom at a 2016 fund-raiser

Here are some key dates in Lady Gaga's life.

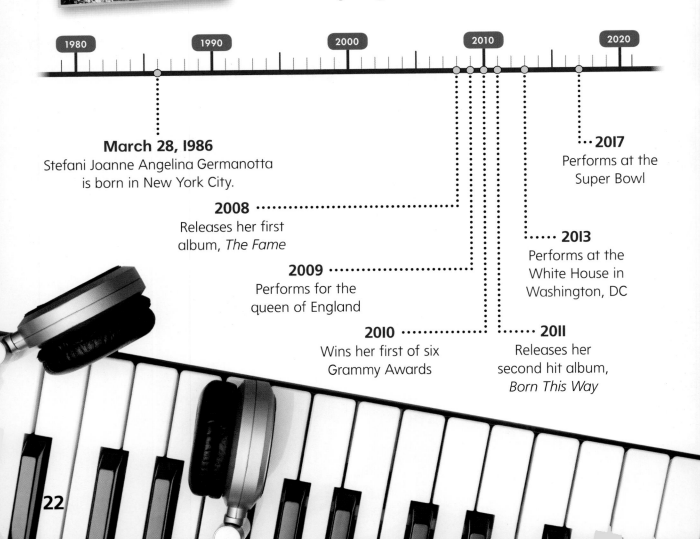

1980   1990   2000   2010   2020

March 28, 1986
Stefani Joanne Angelina Germanotta
is born in New York City.

2008
Releases her first
album, *The Fame*

2009
Performs for the
queen of England

2010
Wins her first of six
Grammy Awards

2011
Releases her
second hit album,
Born This Way

2013
Performs at the
White House in
Washington, DC

2017
Performs at the
Super Bowl

22

Glossary

charts (CHARTS) nickname for lists that rank popular music

duet (DEW-et) a performance by two singers

foundation (foun-DAY-shuhn) an organization that supports or gives money to help people

Grammy (GRAMM-ee) an award given each year for the best music

inspired (in-SPY-yurd) moved to do something creative

musicals (MYOOZ-ik-uhlz) plays that include singing and dancing

Index

Read More

Doeden, Matt. *Lady Gaga: Pop's Glam Queen (USA Today Lifeline Biographies).* Breckenridge, CO: Twenty-First Century Books (2012).

Yasuda, Anita. *Lady Gaga (Remarkable People Biographies).* New York: Weigl (2012).

Learn More Online

To learn more about Lady Gaga, visit

www.bearportpublishing.com/AmazingAmericans

About the Author

Born and raised in New York City, E. Merwin is a writer who much admires Lady Gaga's independence. She also applauds her rise to fame!